THE SLUG

For Henri,
but only when he has a cold

Library and Archives Canada Cataloguing in Publication

Gravel, Elise
[Limace. English]
        The slug / Elise Gravel.

(Disgusting critters)
Translation of: La limace.
ISBN 978-1-77049-656-9 (paperback)

        I. Slugs (Mollusks)--Juvenile literature. I. Title.
II. Title: Limace. English. III. Series: Gravel, Élise.
Disgusting critters.

QL430.4.G7213 2016   j594'.3   C2015-906949-1

Published simultaneously in the United States of America by Tundra Books of Northern New York,
an imprint of Penguin Random House Canada Young Readers, a Penguin Random House Company

Library of Congress Control Number: 2013953638

English edition edited by Samantha Swenson
Designed by Elise Gravel and Tundra Books
The artwork in this book was rendered digitally
Printed and bound in China

www.penguinrandomhouse.ca

8 9   23 22 21

Elise Gravel

THE SLUG

tundra

Ladies and gentlemen, let me introduce

THE SLUG.

The slug is a mollusk, like the snail,
but it doesn't have a

SHELL.

There are

MANY

SPECIES

of slugs.

Sea slugs

Rub-a-dub-dub, one *slug* in a tub.

Freshwater slugs

Land slugs

Abandon ship!

Land slugs are the ones we'll talk about in this book.

The slug has two pairs of

TENTACLES

on its head. The upper ones are eyes, and the lower ones are for smelling and tasting.

I see you! You're a kid and you smell like broccoli!

Its tentacles are

RETRACTABLE,

which means that the slug can pull them
inside its head when it senses

The slug
BREATHES
through a hole on the side of its body.

Everyone's impressed when I do that.

The slug

MOVES

by contracting the muscles
on its belly. Its belly is called a

FOOT.

The slug's whole body is covered in

MUCUS,

a thick and slimy liquid (kind of like snot!). It has to stay in humid areas, such as under stones or flower pots, so it doesn't dry out.

The mucus is very important because it helps the slug move by creating a

SLICK SURFACE.

It also acts like glue to help the slug climb up things like trees and walls.

What a HUGE slug!

When it senses danger, the slug produces extra mucus so it becomes more

SLIPPERY

and can more easily escape its

PREDATORS.

To find a
PARTNER
and have babies, the slug follows another slug's mucus trail.

Just like the earthworm, the slug is male and female at the same time.

The slug lays its eggs in a hole in the ground or under a rock or piece of rotten wood.

BABY SLUGS,

tiny and transparent, will hatch in a few weeks.

The slug eats plants and mushrooms. Farmers and gardeners don't like slugs because they eat their

LETTUCE.

But slugs play an

IMPORTANT

role in the environment. They help to break down old or decaying plant and animal matter and turn it back into important nutrients for the soil.

So next time you meet a slug, be nice. Share some of your

SALAD

with it.